I0233666

by
Khristian E. Kay

Poetry

The Echo
of Rose Petals

khristian e kay

SFUMATO

2012

The Echo of Rose Petals

Copyright ©2012 by Khristian E. Kay

ISBN #978-0-9787444-3-4

All Rights Reserved

For more information on the author see:
www.khristianekay.com

Printed in the United States of America. No part of this book
may be used or reproduced in any manner whatsoever without
written permission except in the case of brief quotations
embodied in critical articles or reviews. For further
information please address the publisher.

Some of the poems in *The Echo of Rose Petals* originally
appeared (sometimes in different versions) in Verse
Wisconsin, Marquette Journal, One Vision, and The Rolling
Thunder Quarterly amongst others

Grateful acknowledgement is given to the editors of these
publications for permission to reprint them here.

The lyrics: *"eddies in the dust of rage"* excerpted from the
Bruce Cockburn song *"Pacing the Cage"* © 1996 Golden
Mountain Music Corp. And *"Somewhere in America"*
excerpted from the Was (Not Was) song *"Somewhere in
America There's a Street Named After My Dad"* © 1988
Universal Music Publishing Group.

SFUMATO books are printed in the USA.

First Edition: January 2012

10   9   8   7   6   5   4   3   2   1

for

josie

Publishing a volume of verse
is like dropping a rose petal
down the Grand Canyon
and waiting for an echo.

Don Marquis

The Echo
of Rose Petals

khristian e kay

Poems

Eddies in the dust of rage

The Adventures of Nerd Boy

Eddies in the dust of rage

It's not polite to stare

Emmett's mother had it right
Not letting her son go quietly
She made a stand opening the casket
Showing her mutilated son
Showing the *humanity* of it all
"Look! Look at what they did to my son!"
"Look!"

Some of us did
Out of fear – conformity
Some out of spite
Some concern
But most of us turned our backs on Emmett's mother

On all mothers who seek justice
For the killing of their children.

Even if they have pictures

No matter what they tell you
No matter how they beg
Do not – I repeat – Do Not
tell people the truth
People do not really
want to know the truth
Lie - make up shit if you have to
But do not ever tell them the truth
They prefer their fantasies
They prefer their make-believe
safety net webbed about them
suffocating tightly
like the larder of a spider

If you tell people the truth
they'll just crucify you
Hang you from some tree
and then make shit up about you

Home Truths

Let's play truth or dare
or just dare because
nobody tells the truth anymore
If what you seek is truth
You can find the truth
However you can't see the truth
standing in front of you
Face the truth -- the ugly truth
is you can't handle the truth
Truth hurts, doesn't it?
How about the truth this time?
The truth is
while you live tell the truth
and shame the devil.
Truth be told
only children and fools tell the truth.
The worst thing about being lied to
is knowing that you are not worth the truth
Fear the truth
for the truth will set you free
If the truth were known

All I ever wanted was the truth
the unvarnished truth
The Gospel truth
The naked truth

But at the moment of truth
bend the truth stretch it
The hardest thing about searching for the truth
is that sometimes you find it.
Because the truth isn't far behind
for nothing could be further from the truth
Look into my eyes therein lies the truth
there must be a kernel of truth in there
somewhere a grain
because your eyes always tell the truth
You can run from the truth but you cannot hide
Because there is no escaping the truth
Tell the truth the whole truth and nothing but the truth

but be economical with the truth
Because the greater the truth, the greater the libel.
Sometimes, truth just isn't good enough
Sometimes truth is stranger than fiction

When you have eliminated the impossible,

whatever remains, however improbable,

must be the truth.

And a lie told often enough becomes the truth

Ain't that the truth!

And the truth will out

Honesty is the best policy

But there ain't no truth in that

I Am Opinionated

You are right
I am opinionated
I'd go so far as to say I'm
prejudiced, discriminatory
an elitist even
a bigot, biased
oh yes I am
against anything ignorant
against anyone uneducated

I don't mean the hallowed halls of
academia nor conformity
where the goal seems to be to
regurgitate what the "in power"
has to proclaim

no I mean ignorant of
conversant thought
the truths we hold self evident
in alienable
those histories left unwritten

You cannot beat the system

I have been often told this
Sometimes by my father whose
Proud countenance sometimes
Overshadowed his jealousies
His nurtured tortures of guild
And repose and inadequacies
Or so I espoused in my impetus youth

I can and I will

You can't beat the system

Authority voices would rain over my head
Rallied in their thirst for control
Thirst because we will do anything
Drink anything swallow anything
To stay alive it is a need Maslow's first
The foundation of all existence and
The foundation for all what we deem important

Hunger we can live with

Hunger is something I like my father tried

To make sure my our children never suffered

But sometimes thirst gets in the way

Despite my father my thirst for knowledge

Put me out of the garden out into the desert

The Poor fools go hungry the Wise ones fast

You can't beat the system

Tell me what to do

The truth will set you free but most people fear their freedoms.
They want to be told what to eat what to think what to be
whom to marry or date what choices they should bear to craft.
When given choices they follow others, celebrities.
We do as taught. Perhaps the aristocracy perhaps
revolutionaries will lead us, but blind we follow.
Even our leaders follow: they follow what their followers
or what they think their followers want for them to swallow.
When given a choice we say we seek wisdom but we look
to the tabloids, hand bills and other gossip magazines;
listen to the media, advertisements, radio;
permission, vindication, it's absolution we seek.

What would you do? What should I do? Tell me, I want to prove
my individual uniqueness. Tell me what to do

"Hey how come you're not watching the game?"

it's difficult to make out who is who
in the slip of blood and mud
where my hand ends and the
flesh of my brothers begin

we all are numb
from the visage from the
play this time around we are not
privy to the shots

I find this fact interesting
how at one time we had people
volunteer their service their
lives as war
correspondents

how we watched the bodies and
bravado come home
in boxes draped with flags
rows of boxes football fields long

Our children, our fathers
our brothers
and now, now...

there is no solemn taps or dance
we envision this
the caskets lowered in reverence
each draped with the universal symbol of American Democracy
American Freedom
the representative service men
providing the appropriate starched
creased salutation
no they are not lowered by the hands of their companions
they are lowered teamster like
crates lifted with a Wisconsin Lift fork truck
moved from plane to dock
cataloged by an exhausted yawning electronic clipboard
like we were signing for some plain wrapped package
from eBay

"hey how come you're not watching the game?"

36 months 3 weeks 4 days 17 and a half hours

I sit here my hat in hand
this hat worn back and tilted to the side
made me the dashing -- the Mack
the baddest brother on the block
how stupidly it sits wringing in my hands
how stupidly I sit

36 months 3 weeks 4 days 17 and a half hours

inside
inside I ain't nobody's bitch

I hold no markers I pay my debts no one is going to own me
inside I killed a man

I didn't even know him
with my bare hands these hands
wringing this stupid hat

I sit here and I want to say
"nobody owns me"

he never did me wrong
but I killed him 'cause I hold no markers
I pay my debts

36 months 3 weeks 4 days 17 and a half hours

look I'm a petty b and e
broken windows and cheap locks
I'm not even good at it
that's why I was in
a drugstore cowboy for my
girls desire fix her up fixed her good
I hold no markers
I ain't nobody's bitch

they tell me down at the state building
that a job application is a legal document
if I lie on it I break the law
and I go back inside

if I tell the truth

when I tell the truth
you dismiss me file me away
like yesterday's trash -- I know what
you think of me...
of course I do
but I ain't nobody's bitch

I fought my way
the petty b and e thief
37 stitches to close up my face
another 25 across my chest
3 screws in my jaw
a pin in my fist
inside I ain't nobody's bitch

but I sit here begging
my hat in hand begging
from a marker from some fat fuck
sitting sweating in his ill fitting
bathrobe

telling me I owe him
I owe him for this chance
this opportunity

36 months 3 weeks 4 days 17 and a half hours

inside I ain't nobody's bitch
outside
out here
I'm everybody's

Are We There Yet?

"Don't make me come back there…!"

You've heard those words
You've probably spoken them

I have said *these* words
riding along in the Chrysler Town and Country
Dad his cigarette hanging from the corner of his mouth
"I'll pull this damn car over right now!
Is that what you want? Well?
I asked you a question! Answer me!"

Are we there yet?

This was our mantra over and over
a cadence embossed in the sticky
vinyl suicide jumper seats
my brother and I
jamming our fingers
through the weather stripping
permanently damaging the car

like millions of other children who'd
force their fingers through the back window
hanging limply as if dad had
rolled the windows up on our fingers
purposely to keep us in line

Are we there yet?

back to front to dad's "*don't*
make me come back there!" or
"*I can turn this car around right now!*"
or …

To my own kids' hourly chime in

"*I'm hungry*"

This is their mantra
"*I'm hungry*
There's nothing to eat"

Even though here in the land of plenty
here there is always plenty of food

"No you're not!" I yell "You have no idea what hunger is"
Hunger to you is the fact that you have not eaten
a bag of chips or a chocolate bar
in the last 15 minutes
you haven't had your daily dose
of Snickers and Red Bull
That is not hunger -- hungry is not having eaten
for the last 15 days
hungry is not being able to hold down a piece of bread
because food has become a foreign entity
to your weakened stomach
hungry is where your own stomach acids
begin digesting the lining
when you cannibalize yourself from the inside
where food has actually become
a poison your body must reject
not choose to…

hungry is not knowing where or when or how or
if ever you will eat again
hunger is not a stomach growling from the emptiness
it is the pain of extension the pressure of distension
where the emptiness has been filled with…

Are we there yet?

At the end of the 19th century
food, hunger, sustenance was the talk
of all of the sciences
how by the end of the 20th century hunger
would be eradicated
foodstuffs plentiful and cheap and nutritious
at one time Kellogg's refused to add sugar
to any of their products
for sustenance should be healthy
good for you
the 20th century has come and gone

We are the land of plenty

so plentiful that we are actually eating ourselves
to death
we burn our excess foodstuffs
let the fruit rot on the vine
in the orchards
we create sport out of killing
animals – not to eat – but to play
with our food
we bury it drown it destroy it
to protect the economy
to protect our profits

all the while we stuff the equivalent of sawdust
animal by-products covered with syrupy sauces
into our bellies

we are the only country in the world
who forcibly and deliberately starve ourselves
from our excess
we surgically modify our bodies

we take pills milkshakes powders chemicals
we puke out our excess
we have recreated the aristocracy
arrogance of Ruben's world

how beautiful is that?

Once when it was fashionable
or it got your picture on the cover
these musicians got together
to teach the world about hunger
"feed the world" they sang

the world is still hungry

"feed the world"
they profited by

hundreds of years later
we are unhealthier than when we were
ignorant farmers in the land of plenty

How far do we have to go?

How many of us will we kill?

feed the world

Aren't we there yet?

Government Cheese

Government cheese don't melt
The trick is to slice it up in little matchstick pieces
Then chop those up into little bits
The cubes mix with watery macaroni
That way with powdered milk
At least you have the illusion of blending

You are forced to be creative
Rice is a formidable staple there
Must be 1001 ways to eat rice
Add cinnamon, sugar and hot water
and again powdered milk -
breakfast! or add a package
of dehydrated mushroom soup mix
and – wild mushroom pilaf!
or a mystery can of vegetables
a can of cream of chicken soup
powdered milk - a chicken casserole
fit for the king
fresh salmon is a newly opened can

you can mix that with instant

mashed potatoes and powdered milk

heat some bacon grease in the pan

and fry up some salmon cakes

and cakes! pancakes and grape jam

mainstays of the hungry cupboard

as are eggs eggs incomparable only to rice

in its many incarnations

fried egg sandwiches, egg salad

sandwiches, hard boiled – soft boiled

poached and shirred with toast

there is no such thing as stale or

leftover bread crust and heels

are delicacies slathered with grape jam

or chopped and mixed into a meat

loaf to make hamburger

stretch across meals

which leaves leftovers for days

sliced cold and thin with onion

and ketchup between day old discount

bread: the beggar's sandwich

topped with a slice of government cheese

I Am the Teacher

How come we were never taught this?

How come no one ever told us the truth?

Because we are like children
innocent in our beliefs
content in our ignorance

tell us a bed time story daddy
keep the monsters at bay

tell us a story where the endings are happy
where all of the girls are princesses
and all of the boys are kings

You are right
I am opinionated
it is my duty
my mission
to educate

to erase ignorance

to develop thinkers

I am the teacher

and your children come to me.

The Adventures of Nerd Boy

Begin first with nobility

Begin first with nobility
not that which comes with our station
defined by birthright or by purchase

to be noble is a circular argument of logic
nobleness cannot exist in a vacuum
one needs a standard to measure by
to be noble without witness
is to be irreverent, difficult
uncaring, deliberate
but to insist on witness one defeats the
whole ideology of what it is to be noble

if you are noble and no one realizes it
are you then just another arrogant asshole?

Christmas Eve 2001

I was standing in her doorway
through guile, sophistication or seduction
I knew I was taking advantage of her situation
She smoked a lady menthol from the kitchen
her waitress uniform still smartly crisp
after a long tenuous shift
I pulled out 2 bills from my clip and placed them
on the Formica counter in front of her

I quoted an old blues song:
"I'll pretend to be your husband if
You pretend to be my wife tonight..."
Her face twisted from curious whimsy but
it was nothing she hadn't heard before
She snubbed her smoke into a dirty plate
and stuffed the bills down her ample cleavage
she waggled her finger in my direction almost
in resignation she said "OK, follow me"
and I followed her to the bathroom

she wiggled her pantyhose down
around her soft shapely thighs
then hopped up onto the vanity slowly rolling
the nylon off her long languid legs
seductively tapping her feet to my
shoulders, chest and chin

I moved to embrace myself between those legs
And she dropped down into my arms and turned
her back dropping her hose into the sink and turning
on the tap her eyes catching mine in the mirror

"You cheap duplicitous bastard!
I suppose we're staying in all night too?
You could at least take me out for a nice dinner."
She turned off the tap and it continued to drip,
"And can't you do something about this leak?
For months drip-drip-drip all night long"

She let down her hair and turned to me brushing it purposefully
"Oh that's right you are too busy gallivanting about
to take care of the essentials like a real man –
we wouldn't have to live like this

if you would have done something with your life...

oh I know – If only: You had a break – If only:

They appreciated you – If only: Daddy had accepted you...

Why don't you do something useful and take the garbage out –

I'm sure you could be successful at that..."

Little Red Headed Girl

This is kind of like that experience
that time back at school with Linda Wesner
You know…

Linda: she was that pretty redheaded girl
y'know the one who was the raison d'etre and bane
of Charlie Brown's existence
We all know that girl
our own pretty redheaded girl
Maybe she wasn't Linda maybe she didn't have red hair
and maybe she wasn't a girl at all
maybe she was that suave chevalier guy - Phil Nick
The highschool boy who was the raison d'etre
or bane of your existence

This was when the pretty redheaded girl
smiled at me and so I go to school
and make a fool out of myself everyday
because the pretty redheaded girl smiled at me

And now I'm trying to get her attention
And really she is a sweet girl
not meaning to be devious or anything
and she smiles more laughs at my jokes
she says something in passing like
"If I didn't have a boyfriend blah blah blah"

Then one day she doesn't have her boyfriend
and I hear this news and go like
"oh yes! "

In school I do my best jester routines
for the pretty redheaded girl who smiled at me
And she sees me and begins to wonder about
all of this attention being lavished and why
am I being so weird and then
it dawns on her: "If I didn't have a blah blah blah"
And she gets to thinking
'Did he think I was serious? '
No? Yes? No… Because see
she wasn't serious
this was just something pretty redheaded girls say

to weird nerd boys
Knowing it would never come true
Everybody knew it would never come true
except obviously nerd boy
But everyone knows that pretty redheaded girls
Don't date nerd boys
Especially nerd boys even though
They order corsages
and even though there were two tickets for the
"You light up my life" or
"Castles in the Sand"
themed prom everybody knew

and even though dad had put on his
best cardigan the hunter green one with the
burgundy and tan stripe down the left
side with that crazy 1950s be bop stitching
fluer de lis everybody knew

I mean why in the world would he ever
think that she: the pretty redheaded girl
would find him a suitable suitor
I mean really

So even though the pretty redheaded girl

who smiled at you was a good girl

(except for that one time under the bleachers with Phil

But that was just the one isolated incident)

And she wasn't mean

And she wasn't devious

she realizes that she needs to distance herself

that she needs to devise a plan

to make nerd boy go away

since nerd boy could not read the social clues

And the signs and followed her about

nipping at her ankles

She had to distance herself from him

and even though his best friends were hiding behind

the evergreen shrubs next to the porch

but out of the light

and mom whipped up her special

simulated crab dip with cream cheese and Raasch's

homemade cocktail sauce fresh from the jar

nerd boy knew

that when she made this compliment

It was not even a half-hearted gesture
Because everyone in the world knows
that she would never go out with a nerd boy
especially nerd boy

so even though he had rented his burgundy tux
with the hot pink piping from the Sears "Fine Young
Gentleman's Store" and buffed his
burgundy and cream platform saddle shoes
nerd boy knew he wasn't going to the prom
with the pretty little redheaded girl or
anyone else

And therefore when the pretty redheaded girls say
"If I didn't have a boyfriend I would be all over you."

It's just something seems safe to say

yeah this is kind of like that.

Aimee always took her time

Aimee always took her time
her long slender fingers
self-manicured pulling and digging
Not the French style
where clean nails are implied
by a fresh coat of white
paint or polish which
lies beneath the paint
but with the pared oily smoothness
of nails working in care products
into the scalp
I would watch her reflection
against the many mirrors
An infinite number of Aimees
all massaging scalps in unison
I'd watch the tilt of her chin the thin
crooked smile through pursed lips
when she was concentrating on
accurate measurements

How her fingers wore her scissors
like magnificent and exotic rings
her long fingers pulling hair up and out to
snip away her nails scratching
into the scalp
Once she caught my gaze
there through a reflected incarnate
of Aimee her eyes crystalline gun barrel blue
pools teeming swirling and I
caught with my thoughts unzipped
and exposed darted my gaze
away fearful and ashamed

She broke my heart the day she
went for a ride with that guy
who held her eye through the glass

She called me a misogynist

Me of all people!
I love women!

I have always been a vocal supporter of women's rights
I still have my ERA buttons!
I marched in their damn parades
went to their male-bashing feminist poetry readings
My friends would say "Hey!
Come on out with us were going to the club,
pick up some chicks…"
I'd say "no thanks
I'm going to a woe-myn rally"
They'd shake their heads and spend their cash
I never spent a dime
Ok maybe a book or two or another pin
But I never went home alone

Funny thing about those male bashing feminists
they always wanted to be on top.

Serialized Smut

Being a poet is not as romantic as it was in the romanticized era
where a traveling troubadour would have laurels thrown at his
feet
Not Laurel Bastion – but laurels of accolades

Back when the writing of poetry meant something manly
meaty, worthwhile, 'mad, bad and dangerous to know'
When orgies of poetry were held – the broad stroking of genius
by Byron, himself master of his manor,
Byron would have an orgy of words
that lasted 3 wet days and nights which would give birth
to Mary Godwin's little boy Frankie – The Good doctor Polidori
would reincarnate Byron's Augustus Darvell , and create the
romantic Night walker genre we still glory in/as The Vampyre
Shelley would conceive his Hymn to Intellectual Beauty
Lives were created, loves glorified, and genres explored
This was poetry

Now it is as if we have to make excuses
to boast of other peculiar machismo

Swing the pendulum a polar opposite arc
for deft macho compensation

 "What do you do?"
-*I write poetry.*
"You write what …?"
-*ah poetry*
"Poetry? Like Roses are red..?"
-*well, yes sort of*
"Oh…"

No you have to swing that pendulum
like a dismembering axe
swing it down to cleave in a singular motion
quick clean and with just enough gore
"What do you do?"
-*me? Oh I'm a poet*
I write poetry
"Poetry? Like roses are…"
yeah
-*that and serialized smut*

Sabbatical

I met this woman once
In a bar in Spokane
I told her I was a runaway monk
A long story about taking a sabbatical
From seminary school
To hitchhike around the country
It was a safe cover as any

She took me home

Sometime around noon she rolled over
Sized me up from under her flop of
Blonde hair

She sighed
"I should have gone to work…"

Valentine's Day at the corner drug store

Pack of Winstons

Hermetically sealed tuna sandwich

Mouthwash

Large can of Red Bull

A single silk rose

Heart shaped box of chocolates

Singing gorilla in NASCAR hat

Filled Valtrex prescription

A card that says *"I forgot..."*

I can make you love me

A bouquet of fresh wildflowers
Some toasted Brie en Croûte
Fresh strawberries and brown sugar
A bottle of St. Michelle sparkling wine

A collection of Marvin Gaye's Greatest Hits
Long white tapered beeswax candles
Sears' 12 volt Die Hard with jumper cables
A pair of powder free latex gloves

A 12 by 20 plastic tarpaulin
Two rolls of industrial strength duck tape
A hand full of prescription Ambien
A mop a bucket a gallon of bleach

Planned Obsolescence

Marriage is nothing more
than planned obsolescence
A method of stimulating
a lover's demand through
promises broken and
worn out from
monotony or monogamy
whichever comes first
in outmoded and
overused desires
or limited use
incorporating relational
features that will
certainly fade or wear
thin of favor and
patience in a shortness
of time inducing lovers
to consume their love:
wit, soul and presence
and most unequivocally

shop around for

a newer, different

more efficient

guileful lying model

To make fun of

This is my story my journey of trials and tribulations
my curriculum vitae – life's work as it were
those experiences which shaped my meaning those
events of my educational awareness my adventures
First, I have to tell you about Cheryl Paul
a pretty girl I grew up with throughout primary
and secondary school too rock and roll earthy
for my teenage sensibilities. By my adult standards
she was a hot little number with long straight hair
parted in the middle who wore that 1970's uniform
of tight jeans and polyester button tops
accented with homemade feather earrings and blue eye
shadow She was also experienced in many ways in life
style choices that I was not -- but purported to be
And as that monumental herd of individuality – the teen
ager is wont to do, accompanied by that 1970's anthem
of going our own way, we flocked together in our
cliques of carbon copy individuals going our own unique ways
in a symmetrical sameness distinct and radical
I thought I was cool, in, or "it" as established by the
random rankings of the American teenager fitting

in with this group or that but not with this one
etcetera etcetera and except for being mixed in classes
over the school years neither Cheryl nor I belonged
to each other's clique so I was hormonally surprised
the day Cheryl signed my yearbook with the open ended
invitation: "We let this year slip by without getting together,
let's not let it happen again this summer…"
– *getting together* -- I could almost hear her purring
those words out of her pen And I entertained those thoughts
often "oh yeah" "Who's got it?" "Who's the man?" but
nothing ever came of Cheryl's hinting as life has its
course to take and interrupts the well made hopes and fantasies
So it would be many years later when a friend of mine
would read through one of my old yearbooks and find
Cheryl's invitation and proceed to laugh. Intrigued
I queried what was so funny about my yearbook – fears
of an embarrassing teen photo or the likes coming to a head
And she commented on "This Cheryl Paul, what she wrote.
My friends and I used to write this almost exact same thing
in the yearbooks of the geeks and nerds: to make fun of them
to see which ones would think it serious – to see who would
try to take us up on it. It was a school girl thing, kind of mean
now that I think about it, but it was way funny at the time."

I looked at the passage all my testosterone furies
once again rising with my imaginary trysts spent with Cheryl
and the sudden chilling deflation as my friend and I
came to the same understanding "I thought you said
you were one of the cool ones in school but
according to Cheryl you were just a nerd..." And suddenly
this became the standard by which I weighed my life
the lens I reviewed my adventures all of those moments,
all of those experiences when I thought I was on
top of the world, when I thought I was cutting the edge
of a new pathway to Coolsville the Poet the Hipster
the storytelling adventurer I was really taken and
received by everyone through the eyes
of Cheryl Paul: as a nerd to make fun of

Somewhere in America

A few minutes more

To close one's eyes
In a 90 mile an hour freefall
bask in the morning sun
cocooned by a blanket of dew laden
wind circling and splaying
wisps of oil, lilacs fragrant on the tongue
or for the lucky moment of garlic mustard
wafting across the meadow a taste of
slow tractor/combine churned manure
weighing heavy in the cleaved fields
the sudden travails of a creek drenched valley
dampening the air in cold assassin shroud
once again the glory warmth
breaking through the canopy with
bowing lilies and obeisant hollyhocks
reverent in their sun drunk columns
sentinels marking the way
to close one's eyes
to bask in the sun
a few minutes more

Favorite Roads

My Favorite Roads are ashen
a chalky white of patched
and cracked arthritic asphalt
aged and bleached
there is no centerline
no paint no makeup just
raw flesh under a midday sun
no defined lines limiting access
but rather following the collective
observable rules
of good conduct and neighborly
jurisprudence
specifically for the polite travelers
the vagabonds trespassing moments
these are not the shiny black roads
the glistening star lights on a sable curtain
these are lifelines like varicose veins
warped and stoic and telling
the Braille staccato of farm implements
and tractors of horses and bikes and
children skipping couples walking
over the sticky tar patches
plastered like gum or pine sap in

the crease of wounded trees
these roads tell stories
experienced and weathered of time
and life of legacy and inheritance
of history whispered through the wind

Rustic Roads

I wish you
had seen the flurry of orange carpet take flight
drifting a lazy smoke of Sulphur Moths
twirling a slow motion whirling dervish
alight in the dust devil updrafts waning and
coating my view breaking waves afore me
with some invisible prow and then closing
in around pounding a fluttering encircling embrace
encompassing like of a salt water surf
still-life surfing at the epicenter of a wake like
a mad butterfly equinox

I wish you

had witnessed the amorous skunks taking the Beatles

to heart propagating in the early morning sun oblivious

to the man made rumble of fossil fuel combustion

in a civil evolutionary fusion in the crunch of gravel

paws padding gentle nest making patters

low mews imperceptible in the sequential candescence

the double backed white stripe

pointing a different path down the highway

one taken many times but each unique and

singular in their moments

I wish you

had ridden with me the sinewy roads through the kettles

winding and serpentine under the deciduousness

and nettles of a Wisconsin autumn

your arms across my chest more embrace than

security a symmetrical gyro in pirouette

wheeling the heated congress of flexing rubber

onto the lithe impassioned tarmac

the wind a lover tearing and pulling at your hair

wafting crisp like fermenting apples sweet and

chilled in the kiss of cider

I wish you

had experienced the thrill of one hundred thirty mile winds

on top a steel steed rocket slaloming the center line

a streaming consciousness provoking poetic

the western dusk driven skies

through a thousand years of glacier etched

pointillism landscapes painted with

the staccato brush of prairie grass and cattails

and river rust clay a retronym shaped and formed

with a willowing sallow breath as I ride

alone off into the sunset

Old Genz

The sign says "Dead End"
it is an unassuming turn
off of a younger Genz that
ovals itself off of Ski Slide Road

But the road dissects the farm
reaching around the back 40
a pleasant detour through the moraine

The children will abandon their play
of skip rope and castle invading or
Corvair racing from atop their
swingset masts

The adults will leave their wash waving
in the wind, horses momentarily unbrushed
their chores kept at bay for the
time being and run up the grassy
wild daisy covered slope
with a wave or smile at the strange sight
of travelers encroaching this path

Their bewilderment belying any
fear or discontent a shout out of a "hey do"
full of curiosity and life

Proving once again that the government
doesn't have a grasp on its citizenry

House of Poems

The rafters burn last
but they also burn hottest
their brittle and aged supports
old couplets stored for
keepsake in antiquated stanzas
tinder for the flames
like morning glory tendrils
reaching up and out
feasting metered in dissonance
breaching dormer windows
Ash falls thick grey flakes
drifting lazily in the night
against the inferno updrafts
sable clipper sailcloth
billowing under full rig
Each window glows its last
fiery breath a light a beacon
for traveling wordsmiths
in the distance warning away
do not venture to this house
as walls like pages in a book

curl on edge in burnt discord ply

upward and inward smoldering

the glued words and separating

their meaning extinguished in allusion

There is nothing here but conceit

burning rhymes lit and brilliant all

but forgotten in the scattered rhythm

ash white and glowing in the night

falling gently towards the ground

Oblivious of the soot streaked faces

faces belonging to these embers

the poet points to the flakes

the final residue of semantics and says

"look momma, snow"

Big Bang Theories

Hawking says it begins this way
a thought expressing itself in the
darkness of nothing: "no thing"
and then exploding itself
across the vast expanse of time
we are composites of these
deposits - particles shooting
out our momentary brilliance
much like the tiny fragments
leftover from this God's eye
burning out in our own atmosphere
a shooting star

I saw a shooting star
arc its way across the sable tapestry
which in profundity is a miraculous
dice game of chance
some etymological particle left
from the Big Bang of the universe
spewing its essence across the
facade of time

and galactic distance

I should not be surprised then

by the toying of the universe

the gamble of irony

that when I see a shooting star

the imagery which comprises it

is that of my old co-worker Duane

who told me about the time

he nailed that Russian exchange student Svetlana

on the rooftop of our building

hanging over the parapet doggy style

so they both could see the twilight

view out across the lake

drawers dropped around

mustard Frye ankle work boots

and as he put it in this most

ecstatic twilight vision

a shooting star burned up its brilliance

at the exact moment he busted his nut

This is what I am left with
every time I see a shooting star
Duane's cleft moon in concert
with the universe's Big Bang
both expending themselves in the darkness

A Dutiful Wife

Move along
there is nothing to see here
nothing to view
no shattering of bones or
ragged wounds to gape at
No nothing that you can see
These wounds here are hidden
swaddled vigilant to my breast
nothing to titillate your senses
nothing to glorify your fantasy
Just a protective shawl drawn tight
across my heart over my beauty
over my delicate features you crave
my gaze that enticed you
I will be quiet, artistic, creative, sullen
spontaneous conservative with my
passions a stole cloak tucked up
around my knees veiled under my pleats
A cloak I will draw across my children
if I choose to have them this mantle
you cannot pierce nor penetrate

No gazing eye can breach this hold
You will see only
what I want you to see
No names or titles no
words for this

I am a dutiful wife
and will never trust you again

The Peanutman

walks through the trees
tossing peanuts for the squirrels who
follow him in his reclaimed clothes
some skirting his coattails while others
climb up his pant legs into his pockets –
all knowing where the stores are kept
warm and dry
he chatters with his friends
those invisible voices his memory trips up
as they clamber about on delicate muscular legs
sometimes sitting on his shoulder as he
retells tales told to those who may remember
and those who may never had existed
sometimes he pulls peanuts from his pockets
biting shells and feeding the squirrels the rich meat
as they cry from his shoulder or deep
inside his pocket
chittering their pleasure or
sometimes they skitter and fight among
one another for the peanutman
who referees these warriors refusing their

share of the prize peanuts

sometimes they scamper around his neck

tails wrapped about his head

or burrowing into his oversized coat nesting

comforting soothing

as he squats at bended knees rocking

on his heels weeping

over the tossed about peanuts scattered

lost in the grass like memories in his mind

Take your little brother with you

Dad says I have to take you swimming with me and my friends
Huh? Well that's cool if you want to come along you can go
We swim by that dam on the Bark at the lower end of
Nemahbin just under the Highway P bridge you'll have fun
There's a spillway slickened with slime we use it like a slide
Just make sure you check for leeches after you go slide down
Those little blood suckers will climb into everywhere if
You know what I mean and after you slide you go under
The bridge be careful there because under bridges y'know
There are all kinds of bees and hornets but they're usually
Not a bother because of all the spiders there are lots
Of spiders really big ones too their webs are everywhere
Spiders so big you'll find blue gills caught in their webs Crayfish
Too they'll pinch your toes if you don't watch out you can also
Swim on the deep side by the reeds as long as you don't step
On the snapping turtles I once saw one snap off a kid's
Finger clean off but you can usually see their bubbles
Coming up from the mud unless of course they're snakes

      but snakes

Won't bother you though they are crazy poisonous it's
The swimming around your legs that is the thing it makes you
Jump and then they strike and on the deep end you got Garfish
They are pretty harmless fish even though they've a mouth like
A crocodile all sharp teeth like needles they eat worms so
Be careful your shorts don't come off because they might mistake
You for a fat dangling worm and you don't lay in the grass
On the bank with all of the ticks those nasty blood suckers
Crawl under your skin and eat you from the inside out and
Then there are the chiggers and Deer Flies

      they'll bite you hard too

Even draw blood, but sure you can come swimming if you want

Will you hear the drums?

I hear the drums in the pater patter
of wolves entreating about the shadows
moon illuminated eclipsed by a
lunacy inherent from the tree line
embers breathe within the blood of fusion
surrounded by the sanctuary of
sacred river stones that altar the fires
with each studied step a dance staccato
in predatory precision rhythm
chanting (howling) each taste of breath in scent

I hear the drums in the maternal flight
of the red tailed hawk with writhing snake
as she ascends above the grassland reeds
in a rhythmic beat with her feathered plumes
slow and deliberate she pounds the air
in deep raptor beats rising with her prey
foraged tightly in her talons the same
as she uses in courtship to grasp on
dihedral wing when planes coincide
her mate's in rare gentle monogamy

I hear the drums in the child-like frolic
of the tiny woodland creatures tapping
their paws chittering against the tree bark
gathering their sacred science and lore
the brush of leaves or crescendo of twigs
to keep time balancing in the rhythm
in oft scurrying woodland business
a gaiety of social production
harmony transposed in seasonal back
beats down strokes and natural elegance

I hear the drums in the dignity of

a people enchanted with tradition

wizened in the ancient stories spoken

from tongue to tongue touch to touch dance to dance

of aged wisdom and youthful candor

of prideful respect promised and betrothed

these human beings native to the soil

oppressed by a greed devoid of honor

beholden to our ancestors of earth

denied the right to freedoms oracled

I hear the drums whispering in the wind
becoming ever faint in the coursing
of time drowned in the river rapids
what history is not recorded is
vanquished by time's subtle machinations
the drums are calling can you not hear them?
the drums are crying can you not hear them?
can you not feel their tears fall in the mud?
can you not hear the drums? Can you not? Now
listen: before they are lost forever.

The Perfect Christmas Poem

Six months into the first
war to end all wars
Some soldiers on
the Western front
Defied their orders
and crossed into
The wasteland
between the trenches

The Germans sung carols
The French brought wine
The Brits a football
They crossed language barriers
and created teams
traded cigarettes and rations
And played a friendly
game of football while
betting souvenirs
on their teammates

With a Camaraderie
demonstrating the likes
of Civility and Humanity
never known again since
Christmas Day, 1914

People who don't know they are dead

and those of us who still seek their approval

She

She once told me …
She tells me a lot
I never get a word in edgewise
She tells me what to think
what to say - who to say it to
She tells me what to wear

Instructs me on how to cut my hair
when to laugh when to cry
when to stand steadfast
She directs my every move
in the kitchen – garage – in the
yard and in bed
She is my muse
my bane of existence

She makes me write
forces me to transcribe
her words in detail with no
forethought or insight of my own
She is poetry

Of Fathers: semantics

You must understand the value of words
their syntax and command their power
to control and define

"Well?" she asked "what would you do?"

"It's not a question I want to answer"
It is not a concept that we should even
Be entertaining -- it is like naming the forbidden

"No we should be talking about this, it is
important it is who we are now."

"It's like seeing the bride in her gown before the
wedding -- it is like..."

"No. It is a reality a fact of life like death
I want to know -- if there are
complications
what are you going to do?"

Complications? Complications?
giving birth having a baby is not *complications*
it is a change in life life arriving
newly born newly aware newly alive

"But what if there were complications?
What are you going to do?"

And this I thought about my hand
resting on your kicking feet
flexing and stretching inside her belly
This I thought about this life inside
this consciousness awareness thriving
and thrashing about impatient to
begin to grow to renew
this tapping against my palm
through the skin that I have caressed and warmed
Of course! I would tell them to save you
we could always have another baby
but save the mother save my wife save the
woman I love

"Of course! I would choose you."

She curled into my arms on my lap
almost purring as you often do
you remind me of her in these many ways

She must have known the truth
She was a very smart woman
and the truth is that I am a good father

better than any husband I could ever be

You scare me

The visions are increasing
You haunt my thoughts
Images perceived or real or desired
I shake them like a woolen rug
Flung over the rail
Pieces or fragments
Of my being dropping off
Floating away
Twisting in the wind
Lost in the earth
Some tangible in my breath
Bits of my soul become
Foreign objects lodged in my lungs
Collapsing them collapsing my reason
Stealing my breath
Stilling my heart

The Adventures of Rat Boy

You were always a queer little boy
I mean that in the archaic sense of
my own historical lexicon meaning
unique different extra-ordinary the
words I grew up with as opposed
to the name you now embrace
with your tales of super human feats
and exploits of speed and flight
and visibility you aligned yourself
with rats I think you identified
with the darkness the scurry of time
and their gentle intelligence
your flock of hair dark in your eyes
some or another blanket tied about
your shoulders derring-do in your
diapered shorts as you'd land from
the couch with a *"da-ta-da!*
I am Rat Boy!"
Now you are not so little

you are not the queer little boy I
could hold in the palm of my hand
rocking you throughout your sleepless
nights afflicted by some fear or sickness
that only I could subside by rocking
and singing low sad songs about your
blue eyes pale in the twilight
perhaps this was the darkness you tried
to hold onto for so many years
slumbering against my neck
my hand at once soldiering you and
caressing your tiny back secure
and wanted and loved
No you no longer are that little boy
you are a man forthright still queer
however now it is on your terms
the colloquial mantle you carry about you
in your furthering defense of truth and
righteousness of becoming
erect and defined substantiated
in a society callous and afraid
You are not that queer little boy
you are my son still wanted and loved

Sleeping with Ghosts

No there's nothing you can do
It has nothing to do with you
I'm sure you are the best but
You cannot fix it
I have been here many times
I know how you will deal with this
You will mock me
You will feel insulted, responsible
And then repudiate me
I could tell you a story
About an accident during the war
Or about a disease that ravages the body
Or the mind or cite an aphorism
Of a life wicked ill spent
I could blame you and leave you
With the mock of disgust
But I will tell you why and you
Will mock me which is easier
Than to believe our energy our spirit
Our soul transcends the boundaries of what
We see, we hear, smell, taste,

What we touch and what we touch
We leave part of us behind, part
Of our soul our energy much
Like fingerprints left on glass
Scraps of our spiritual DNA
Are left on those things we touch
We attach ourselves to, we attach
Our energy to and like a forensic
Scientist I process those scraps of energy
Feel them, taste them, hear them, smell them
On everything they've touched
See them everywhere they've been
With you I am surrounded by their
Essence immersed in their effluvia
These ghosts of our pasts ghosts
Of your love whispering, watching,
Listening… and mocking me

The Dispossessed

They walk among us whispering in our ears
Telling us their fears, their worries
reminding us in the only way possible
controlling us

repeating directions over and over
and over even when we comply

> *wash your hands, lock the door*
> *eat eat drink more, pick at it, scratch it*

We do not get rid of them or shut them up
We learn to ignore the more we ignore
sometimes the quieter they get,
Sometimes…

They are full of advice good or bad not to be ignored
so they whisper in desperation

> *take it take it, touch it, hold it, want it, take it*
> *more you need more, wipe wipe, wash your hands*

They tell us what to think what to say
They know only their monocular vision
their need of great importance
Their legacy

They talk to us in our dreams, our visions
Argue as voices deliberating in our heads

>   *don't go outside, don't go up, don't go fast*
>   *germs, wash, scrub, eat, scratch, run, fight*

We learn to quiet some of the voices
by drink, by smoke, we ignore, we comply
Some settle in and some move on
quiet forever

Others will take their place and in the end in the quiet
We miss them when they are gone

The Fourth World

We are omni-dimensional beings
Experiencing the confines of only 3
This fourth dimension or world
Exists as a spiritual realm
It is the depot between Being and existence

What James Morgan Pryse calls
The world of "general psychic garbage"
For "dead" matter has no place.
The universe is a manifestation of life,
of consciousness,

All that is contained in the universe
is also contained within man.

From the Logos to the very atoms
of material elements.
A sharp distinction must be
made between Being and existence
Logos, the Archetypal world,
is True Being, changeless and eternal;

while existence is a going outward
into the other realms of becoming,
of transformation.

All that the universe contains
is contained also in man.

Analogous with the universe or macrocosm,
man, the microcosm, has the spiritual
the psychic and the physical bodies
In mystical writings these three, together
with the fourth, or perfected vesture

of the Nous, the immortal Self, or mind create
the spiritual, not a body at all, but an ideal,
archetypal form, ensphered, as it were, by
the cycle of incarnations, passing- from
one mortal coil to another.

All that is contained in the universe
is also contained within man.

It is then a fact as apparent to him
as are the cognate facts of birth and death.
That the perfected man is thereby
freed from the necessity physical and
psychic forms – rather another body is

alluded to. It is the form engendered by lust,
it comes into existence only after death
It is a phantasm of such nature as the demons
And "unclean spirits" and the existence of
The metaphysical

All that the universe contains
is contained also in man.

This realm of the in between this holy of
Holies is the Geiger counter by which
We warrant our mythos of knowledge
Of experiencing that of Being the collected
consciousnesses we have gathered

the Builders who whisper schematics
into our awareness the Nous guide
arching the psychic, spiritual and physical
which threads the balance of existence
through Being

All that is contained in the universe
is also contained within man.

It is the Fourth world where we are fallen
Creviced in the abyss of Being and existence
Caught in the realm of lust for physicality
With no regard for experiential knowledge
The omniscient wisdom of the temporal

We haggle and plead barter with our demons
Who are really manifestations of our
own immortal Being lost in the cacophony
of spiritual intellect devoid of light and
the *gnosis* of truth:

All that the universe contains
is contained also in man.

An insolent boy

She said I was insolent I didn't want to be
I don't even know what that means
She was nice and I didn't want her to hit me
I tried to please her but still she told me
I was insolent
She told me to turn the page sideways that that was
How left handed people had to write
Otherwise their hands would smear the ink
leaving blue/black stains on the edge of our palms
I told her *I can't*
And she reprimanded me "You mean you won't!"
I insisted I couldn't
Because if I turned the page the words wouldn't have
Anything to stand on and would fall off the page
Thereby being meaningless and void without form
She said I was insolent
And that she was calling my mother I told her – *you can't*
"Oh I can't can't I?" And she spurred on her heel
No I insisted - *you can't call my mother*
"We'll just see about that now won't we?"

But she didn't hit me like the teachers at my last school
Who said only devils wrote with their left hands and they would
Strike the knuckles of my hand with the metal edge of their rulers
If they caught me – 'thwack'
"You're pledging allegiance to the devil."
'thwack' and the metal edge would cut
"You insolent boy!" – 'thwack'
I didn't mean to be insolent I don't even know what that means
I didn't want to know what it means that's how I rationalized
My 7 year old sensibilities like the day my father
Gathered us around and told us that our mother had
Passed away I didn't know what that meant either
Dad explained in his best way
"Your mother is dead."
Everyone cried then because we knew what that meant
Everything was ok when she had just passed away but because of
me
Now She was dead
I didn't want something bad happening again when
Insolent was explained to me
 - *you can't call my mother.*

"You don't want me calling your mother,

you mean"

no, you can't "and why is that young man?"

She stamped her foot, crossed her arms

And narrowed her eyes at this

Like the two small letter "e"s in the word "see"

One next to the other

Following a slow hiss and my words do not fall off the page

But they do tumble about in a mishmash of acrobatics none

Wanting to stay on the lines really it not being explained to them

And while I did not not learn how to write like the devil

I did learn that people do not want to hear the truth rather

They need to discover truth for themselves

I didn't want to be insolent

I didn't want it to be true - *my mother's dead*

"You dasn't say things like that lest they come true."

She admonished and pivoted away I shrugged – it was true

I'm an insolent boy

You heard me

'You heard me the first time' I can tell by
the sudden square of your shoulders the quick
bristle of your spine erect enough I
could plumb a wall by dropping you from an
arch as a line but I keep these thoughts
to my head I do not wish to engage
provoke or agitate. Why create an
animosity where there is none? I
was only trying to create discourse.
Why tip the balance for favor? I am
merely suggesting timbre seemingly
does reflect upon stature. It is a
compliment for crying out loud! Do you
think that I do not exist within my
own revelry? That my thoughts too are not
carried and bantered about like some ghost
plastic bag caught in a tug of war by
a devil's wind? That my own temporal
vestiges are not themselves lost in some
importance immersed in desire thoughtful

and reflective? How do you know that I
was not also lost in thought? Switching tracks
in some neuron terminal bulleting
an electromagnetic monorail
charging through the axon or galloping
a v-twin rearing up and over the
recesses passing each node "flash" node
"flash" node "flash" node memory layering
upon strobe emulsifying into
focus like a Polaroid. Shape shifting
in mottled hues, tones, caricatures, forms
outlined yet shapeless "flash" synapses fired
neurons stretched across some temporal
highway dendrites hitchhiking like the so
many winter ice stalactites growing
mineral drip by drip - spark by spark - "flash"
by "flash" until a connection cements
a relationship and made glowing and
stretching electric elastic alive
and "flash" Just like that memory races
through the myelin sheath the "flash" of white lines
blending into a singular blurring node
widening vibrating into key in

focus forming an image a phantom
haunting of the past trail-braking dead. And
"flash" like a bulb exploding hot from a
Brownie 127 blinding and
disorienting I'm there sitting in
Mrs. Brodie's 1st grade classroom my stiff
cotton Nehru shirt and a silk scarf worn
like an ascot itching and choking all
gussied up as some eternal nineteen
seventies' Carnaby Street style fashion
icon - All's quiet on the attention
front with the stick-in-the-muds and goody-
two-shoes and the saccharin smiles of all
the pleasers and pets with their undying
love, doing what is expected of them
their conformity and complacency.
This apathy churning inside me like
an Intestinal Crank I jump up on
my desk my voice resonating: "Hey! Hey
wake up! There is no parental rule here.
We are not obligated by some odd
viral nationalistic dictator
to lock-step our toes in line *'put your right*

foot in, put your right foot out.' C'mon snap
out of it! Don't just sit there! Do something,
say something; we are *free* beings. We are
sentient creatures; nymphs of anarchy,
there is no parental more here. There
is no dogmatic doctrine legalese
of confinement. No *'big brother'* watching
authoritarian *'other'* portrait
whipping us in our places – There is no
Milgram sensibility to herd our
mentality. We are the kings and queens
of our own renaissance. We own the day.
The asylum is ours!" These are not the
exact words I say my 7 year old
lexicon not quite sophisticated.
Instead I moan low, growl a wild eyed stare
capturing snap shots all about the room
every direction at every
sight every sound every nuance
every burp, fart, eraser squeaking,
booger slurping, arm raising, primp talking
'wait-your-turn' member of this love commune
with some weird breathy not quite laugh not quite

sigh - more animal than human – but still
the meaning is clear. And "flash" I'm off with
the broken bulbs breaking noses here and
bloodying lips there like the feral beast
that I am surrounded by a mob of
those herd kids chanting "C'mon! C'mon boy!"
I relentlessly strike out and kick at
whatever metaphor I can get my
hands on: "You like to make kids cry? Me too,
c'mon you son of a bitch cry!" And the
pulp of cartilage crumples against my
fist pink and sticky with blood my hands wrapped
about in my fury my truth. Because
"flash" the truth be told I too was in love
with Mrs. Brodie her pretty cotton
mini dress - I can feel the yellow cloth
soft cotton electricity supple
radiating to my testosterone
laden aura "C'mon boy. C'mon!" it
clung to her thighs coming just to the knee
in concert with the Nancy Sinatra
go go boots "flash" But my love is of a
different realm somewhere out there around

that mob edge in some neon flashed motel
room curtains drawn spotlight on the sweat stained
mattress where a Super 8 is peeping
through Ektachrome windows flashing at the
Fellini-esque direction of some low
budget Russ Meyer wanna-be –and "flash"
No bow tie wearing *"Can I carry your*
books?" infatuation here no sir but
big, smothering bouncy kind of love the
kind where there is never enough soap "flash"
And yes I know her husband had just died
people die that is the only truth the
only reality: we live we die
"flash" War will do that it doesn't matter
if you are innocent or not, good or
not, people die, everyday, many
will die I have seen them men, boys, fathers,
sons, mothers "flash" Not enough hot water
to scrub off the legacy of some punk
kid staring out of his neighbor's window
at his own home out of reach across the
lawn wishing for his mommy and "flash" Our
principal died - killed himself – blew his brains

out in the garage "flash" My mother had

a lump – on her throat "flash" His son was killed

in that war too "flash" Anywhere but here

here in any man's pleasuredome "flash" Up

in the rafters of the garage my own

secret pleasuredome smoking shoplifted

cigars where it was so hot you could smell

the two by fours smoldering thumbing through

the old man's Playboys trying to understand

what I see what I feel – the only things

making sense being the Gahan Wilson

cartoons and Shel Silverstein poetry

"flash" Down by the tracks laying pennies and

my head on the rails listening for and

waiting for the trains "flash" I'm supposed to

be taking a nap so I pretend to

be asleep when the sitter comes to the

room to play making sure everything

is pink and tucked in and is in working

order "flash" Mrs. Brodie is crying

collapsing to the floor in wrenching sobs

"flash" My mother crumples on the stairs "flash"

The sitter smothering with that bouncy

wet pink "flash" My fist caked red-handed with
blood and shaking "flash" I want to grab that
big Doofus with the *"I love you Mrs.*
Brodie" grin by the ears and smash his head
into the desk until his world turns pink
bouncy, and smothered in the tabloid of
my world "flash" *'Wait your turn.'* "flash" *'C'mon boy,*
c'mon!' "flash" *'Are you all tucked in?'* "flash" *'Cry*
you son of a bitch!' "flash" *'I love you.'* "flash"
'Don't cry now honey.' "flash" It's not that I
don't understand your indignation it's
just that I feel it is unwarranted –

"What I said was: 'you're kinda short aren't you?'"

11:55

Time is a subjective and elusive maiden

A man-made and hand crafted misconfiguration

Rhythmically marking the de- evolution/composition

Of man's vanity of controlling his environment

Structuring against the wisdom of nature

If we muzzle the wolf we keep the pretense of safety

At the cost of his life trying to dam back time

Dam the cascading waterfall which traps us in flight

Sailing the march of time riding an ark of imaginary command

We are enslaved bound by the machinations of time

Bound by the illusionary role of freedom

Ticking away tick-tock stealing away the moment

How do we know when we are at the abyss the edge

Falling into a precursor to the meridian glory or the

Bewitching hour of haunts and demons?

It is an arbitrary label ambivalent in its distinction

We are being warned, reminded or alarmed –

Destiny has no captain knows no master

Regardless you only have 5 minutes left

Sorry about the mess

What is the purpose of all this?

Why subject you to this pandering meaningless

meandering of my indulgences?

Why waste your time with this selfish

juxtaposition of caricature

of character and style?

Is there a greater wisdom or purpose?

A verbose balm to soothe mental anguish?

Words of morality, a lesson, a truth, a story?

Or just the exploitative excesses of immoral ambiguity?

If you are not outraged
you are not paying attention.

www.KnowB4No.org

AIDS/HIV and other STDs are at pandemic proportions – *are you aware?* The largest "group" contracting these life destroying diseases are America's children, CHILDREN! Children between the ages of 10 and 25: regardless of gender, regardless of socio-economic status, regardless of sexual preferences. *Why?* Without knowledge we are all doomed to die stumbling about in the dark. Become educated, seek your own answers, do not *accept* what you are told, do not *accept* blind allegiance, do not *accept* dogma.

It *is* your life – it is *your* future: *or not* you choose.

Knowledge Before Abstinence

www.ingramcontent.com/pod-product-compliance
Lightning Source LLC
LaVergne TN
LVHW011206080426
835508LV00007B/624

* 9 7 8 0 9 7 8 7 4 4 4 3 4 *